Don't forget to check out these excellent online resources to help you learn more about Educational Psychology!

CD Connection to the "Becoming a Professional" Website

The CD-ROM can be found at the back of your new Woolfolk, Educational Psychology, 9/e text. The "Becoming a Professional" Website is **a tool to help you succeed in the classroom and beyond**. The website contains a wide variety of features that will help you take what you learn in the classroom and use it to get started in your teaching career. The site will **help you:**

- **Prepare for teacher certification exams** by highlighting material commonly found on the exams, providing sign up information, and noting useful study aids;

- **Get your first job** by putting together an impressive resume, portfolio and electronic portfolio, write effective job application letters, and by refining your interviewing skills

- **Perform your job well from the first day** by providing a wealth of time-tested and immediately usable teaching activities, web links, worksheets, and exercises, all developed by expert educators.

Companion Website (www.ablongman.com/woolfolk)

If you visit the Companion Website that accompanies the text (www.ablongman.com/woolfolk) you will find many features and activities to help you in your studies: web links and journaling activities; practice tests; an interactive glossary; and vocabulary flash cards. The website features an extended "Teacher's Casebook" with additional audio, video, and text-based cases and activities. The site also contains examples of classroom work created by children in many content areas students. You will be able to assess these artifacts by linking to the discussion and ideas from the main text.

Praxis Guide

for

Woolfolk

Educational Psychology

Ninth Edition

prepared by

James B. O'Kelly
Rutgers University and Sayreville Public Schools

Boston   New York   San Francisco
Mexico City   Montreal   Toronto   London   Madrid   Munich   Paris
Hong Kong   Singapore   Tokyo   Cape Town   Sydney

To obtain permission(s) to use the material from this work,
please submit a written request to Allyn and Bacon,
Permissions Department, 75 Arlington Street, Boston, MA
02116 or fax your request to 617-848-7320.

ISBN 0-205-39683-6

Printed in the United States of America

10 9 8 7 6 5 4 3 2 1   08 07 06 05 04 03 02

Contents

PART ONE
GENERAL PRAXIS TEST
INFORMATION

Description of *The Praxis Series*®

The Praxis Series® comprises three separate tests: the Praxis I, II, and III. The Praxis I test is also referred to as the PPST or Pre-Professional Skills Test. According to *The Praxis Series* ® homepage on the ETS Web site (http://www.ets.org/praxis/), these three tests are intended to mark three major milestones of teacher development: 1) entering a teacher-training program, 2) licensure for entering the teaching profession, and 3) the first year of teaching. Currently, thirty-five states require prospective teachers to pass at least one of the Praxis tests. Other states and professional organizations (e.g., National Association of School Psychologists) also use the Praxis tests in some form. Information on qualification standards by state and organization is available at: http://www.ets.org/praxis/prxstate.html.

The formats for Praxis I and Praxis II tests include scenarios, case histories, and comprehensive reading. Conceptual knowledge, procedural knowledge, and representations of quantitative information are assessed on the Praxis I, and organizing content knowledge, creating an environment for student learning, and teacher professionalism are assessed on the Praxis II. You can download the national Praxis Series Registration Bulletin at: http://www.ets.org/praxis/prxreg.html. The bulletin provides information necessary to apply for the Praxis I and Praxis II tests. There is a separate registration bulletin for those taking the Praxis II in California, accessible at the same site. The above website also provides individual links to test centers and dates, as well as other registration options.

Praxis I

The PPST assesses basic competencies in reading, mathematics, and writing. The intent is to give students the opportunity to assess basic skills before spending time, money, and energy training to become teachers. For state-by-state passing scores on the Praxis I test, see http://www.ets.org/praxis/prxstate.html.

The Praxis I test can be taken in a traditional paper-based format, at many colleges about six times a year, and at all Sylvan Testing Centers with less than a week's notice. The Praxis I can also be taken as a computer-based test (CBT). The CBT format is tailored to each candidate's performance, and provides different question types and immediate scoring. Computer based tests take two hours per test, allowing time for tutorials and collection of personal information. If your keyboarding or word processing skills are limited, this option is not recommended. If you want to take the CBT, you can call 1-800-853-6773 for a *Prometric* test site near you. Individuals who are deaf or hard of hearing and use a TTY should call the following number instead, 1-800-529-3590. More information about CBT is available at the following site: http://www.ets.org/praxis/prxcbt.html.

The fee for the Praxis I test varies depending on the format and how many tests are taken at once. For more information on both versions of the Praxis I test and a list of CBT testing centers, visit http://www.ets.org/praxis/prxpIoption.html.

The following chart contains the basic data about the Praxis I tests:

Code	Test	Time	No. of Questions	Format	Content	Score Range
10710	PPST Reading	60 mins.	40	Multiple Choice	1. Literal comprehension 2. Critical and inferential comprehension	150-190
10730	PPST Math	60 mins.	40	Multiple Choice	1. Conceptual knowledge 2. Procedural knowledge 3. Quantitative information 4. Geometry 5. Formal mathematical reasoning	150-190
20720	PPST Writing	30 mins.	45	Multiple Choice	Use of English grammar	150-190
		30 mins.		Essay	Requires writing an essay on an assigned topic.	

Praxis II

The Praxis II tests consist of 140 specialty area tests, multiple subject assessments for teachers (test codes 10140 and 20151), and general tests covering principles of learning and teaching. The Principles of Learning and Teaching tests—30522, 30523, and 30524—are where you will encounter questions concerning educational psychology. Therefore, they are the primary focus of this Praxis guide. According to the ETS, the 140 content tests are regularly updated, and several are available in each subject field. Therefore, a state can customize its program by selecting those assessments that best match its own licensure requirements. The ETS website http://www.ets.org/praxis/prxtest.html provides more information on the structure of the 140 content tests. The ETS website http://www.ets.org/praxis/prxstate.html provides specific state requirements for content tests. Because many states norm-reference Praxis scores, passing scores are likely to change often. So, be sure to keep yourself up to date of all necessary information by checking the above website periodically.

The following chart contains basic data about the Praxis II: Principles of Learning and Teaching:

Test Code	Test Name	Time	Number of questions	Format	Topics covered
30522	Principles of Learning and Teaching Grades K-6	2 hours	12 short-answer question and 24 multiple-choice questions	4 case histories, each followed by 3 short-answer question; 24 multiple-choice questions, in two 12-question sections	1. Students as learners 2. Instruction and assessment 3. Communication techniques 4. Profession and community
30523	Principles of Learning and Teaching Grades 5-9	2 hours	12 short-answer question and 24 multiple-choice questions	4 case histories, each followed by 3 short-answer question; 24 multiple-choice questions, in two 12-question sections	1. Students as learners 2. Instruction and assessment 3. Communication techniques 4. Profession and community
30524	Principles of Learning and Teaching Grades 7-12	2 hours	12 short-answer question and 24 multiple-choice questions	4 case histories, each followed by 3 short-answer question; 24 multiple-choice questions, in two 12-question sections	1. Students as learners 2. Instruction and assessment 3. Communication techniques 4. Profession and community

Praxis III: Classroom Performance Assessments

The Praxis III test usually takes place during a teacher's first year of service. According to *The Praxis Series® Tests at a Glance* booklet:

"Praxis 3 classroom performance assessments are used at the beginning teaching level to evaluate all aspects of a beginning teacher's classroom performance. Designed to assist in making licensure decisions, these comprehensive assessments are conducted in the classroom by trained local assessors who employ a set of nationally validated criteria."

Test-Taking Tips

The following test-taking tips are compiled from a variety of sources, including the ETS Praxis guides and students who have taken the Praxis tests.

Before the Test

- Complete many practice tests. Comfort and familiarity with the test format are learned skills. (ETS)
- Work on essay writing skills. You must be able to incorporate the pedagogical content in your essay.
- Study with a friend.
- Create vocabulary drill cards. Start by referring to the chapter reviews and glossary in your textbook. Have a friend drill you on the vocabulary found there. Have your friend mark the terms you don't know. You can create your vocabulary drill cards from those words. Use an 81/2 x 11 sheet folded in half. Put the terms on the left side and the definitions on the right. Writing the information on a drill card will also help you remember the facts. This process will help you with the case studies and provide you with content for your essays. Alternatively, go to the Companion Website for your text book (www.ablongman.com/woolfolk) and click on the Flashcards button for each chapter.
- Be prepared to write responses to classroom scenarios. Readers do not want lengthy answers, so learn to condense information. Be parsimonious!
- Revisit basic mathematics and geography facts for the Elementary Content/Specialty tests.
- Do not plan to leave as soon as you finish the test. You have to stay the entire time. You also will probably need the entire time provided for the essay portion.
- Know how to deal with children's behaviors in the classroom. One essay question asked about handling "copying" in the classroom.
- Go to bed early.

The Day of the Test

- Tests start at the exact time; do not be late!
- You must bring a picture ID to the testing center. (ETS)
- Bring three #2 pencils with erasers. (ETS)
- Wear a watch. (ETS)
- Eat a light breakfast.

- Bring a scientific calculator. (ETS)

- Select a good seat. Do not sit near anything or anyone that will distract you.

- If you are easily distracted, bring a pair of earplugs and use them once the test has started.

- Use your test booklet for scratch paper. No one reviews material written on the test booklet.

- Read through the questions slowly and carefully. Think of a probable answer before you look at the multiple-choice selection.

- If you are taking the pencil and paper test, go through the questions and answer those you are confident about. Take subsequent passes through to answer the rest of the questions with the time remaining. Answer every question; there is no penalty for wrong answers. Note that the CBT (computer-based test) may not allow this strategy.

- For essay portions, start by making an outline in the "notes" space; nothing you write there will be graded. Organize your essay before you begin. The job will be half done before you start. Include a thesis statement, introduction, topic sentence, expansion on the topic, and conclusion. Be sure to double-space your writing so that you can edit if necessary by neatly crossing out and replacing words.

- Keep track of your answers on your answer sheet— make sure you are in the correct sequence. Read topics carefully.

- Stay focused, and do not panic. You are expected to give incorrect answers. Your goal is to pass, not get a perfect score.

Multiple Choice Strategies

- Read the questions carefully. Some words are frequently word traps, including *not, least, except, always,* and *never*. When you see these words, read the question a second time.

- Do not panic if you do not immediately know the answer. Cross off the answers that are definitely wrong. Put all the information you have together and take your best guess. Practice deductive reasoning; construct your own knowledge. Remember, the answer is right in front of you.

- For math questions, do the problem in your head. Cross out answers that are definitely incorrect. Work the problem; you will have already eliminated the "trick" answer.

State-by-State Requirements and Passing Scores

The following chart lists the Web sites that show which Praxis tests are currently required in different states and U.S. territories. Most states are in the norm-referencing phase, and up-to-the minute information can be accessed at http://www.ets.org/praxis/prxstate.html.

Alaska	http://www.ets.org/praxis/prxak.html	Nebraska	http://www.ets.org/praxis/prxne.html
Arkansas	http://www.ets.org/praxis/prxar.html	Nevada	http://www.ets.org/praxis/prxnv.html
California	http://www.ets.org/praxis/prxca.html	New Hampshire	http://www.ets.org/praxis/prxnh.html
Connecticut	http://www.ets.org/praxis/prxct.html	New Jersey	http://www.ets.org/praxis/prxnj.html
Delaware	http://www.ets.org/praxis/prxde.html	New Mexico	http://www.ets.org/praxis/prxnm.html
District of Columbia	http://www.ets.org/praxis/prxdc.html	North Carolina	http://www.ets.org/praxis/prxnc.html
Florida	http://www.ets.org/praxis/prxfl.html	Ohio	http://www.ets.org/praxis/prxoh.html
Georgia	http://www.ets.org/praxis/prxga.html	Oklahoma	http://www.ets.org/praxis/prxok.html
Hawaii	http://www.ets.org/praxis/prxhi.html	Oregon	http://www.ets.org/praxis/prxor.html
Indiana	http://www.ets.org/praxis/prxin.html	Pennsylvania	http://www.ets.org/praxis/prxpa.html
Kansas	http://www.ets.org/praxis/prxks.html	Rhode Island	http://www.ets.org/praxis/prxri.html
Kentucky	http://www.ets.org/praxis/prxky.html	South Carolina	http://www.ets.org/praxis/prxsc.html
Louisiana	http://www.ets.org/praxis/prxla.html	Tennessee	http://www.ets.org/praxis/prxtn.html
Maine	http://www.ets.org/praxis/prxme.html	Texas	http://www.ets.org/praxis/prxtx.html
Maryland	http://www.ets.org/praxis/prxmd.html	U.S. Virgin Islands	http://www.ets.org/praxis/prxvi.html
Minnesota	http://www.ets.org/praxis/prxmn.html	Vermont	http://www.ets.org/praxis/prxvt.html
Mississippi	http://www.ets.org/praxis/prxms.html	Virginia	http://www.ets.org/praxis/prxva.html
Missouri	http://www.ets.org/praxis/prxmo.html	West Virginia	http://www.ets.org/praxis/prxwv.html
Montana	http://www.ets.org/praxis/prxmt.html	Wisconsin	http://www.ets.org/praxis/prxwi.html

The following chart shows which states currently require the Praxis I tests and the Praxis II pedagogy tests. Most states are in the norm-referencing phase, and up-to-the minute information can be accessed at http://www.ets.org/praxis/prxstate.html.

State	10710 PPST Reading	20720 PPST Writing	10730 PPST Math	30522 Grades K–6	30532 Grades 5–9	30524 Grades 7–12
AK	•	•	•			
AL						
AR	•	•	•	•	•	•
AZ						
CA						
CO						
CT	•	•	•			
DC	•	•	•			
DE	•	•	•			
FL	•	•	•			
GA	•	•	•		•	
HI	•	•	•	•	•	•
IA						
ID						
IL						
IN	•	•	•			
KS	•	•	•	•	•	•
KY	•	•	•	•	•	•
LA	•	•	•	•	•	•
MA						
MD	•	•	•			•
ME	•	•	•			
MI						
MN	•	•	•	•	•	•
MO					•	•
MS	•	•	•	•	•	•
MT	•	•	•			
NC	•	•	•			
ND						
NE	•	•	•			
NH	•	•	•			
NJ						
NM						
NV	•	•	•	•		•
OH				•	•	•

State	10710 PPST Reading	20720 PPST Writing	10730 PPST Math	30522 Grades K–6	30532 Grades 5–9	30524 Grades 7–12
OK	•	•	•			
OR	•	•	•			
PA	•	•	•	•		•
RI				•		•
SC	•	•	•	•	•	•
SD						
TN	•	•	•	•	•	•
TX	•	•	•			
UT						
VA	•	•	•			
VT	•	•	•			
WA						
WI	•	•	•			
WV	•	•	•	•	•	•
WY						

PART TWO
CORRELATIONS TO THE TEXTBOOK

General Information about Educational Psychology

What is educational psychology? According to Anita Woolfolk, your textbook author, the goals of educational psychology are "to study learning and teaching and, at the same time, strive to improve educational practice." (Woolfolk 9/e, p.9)

For the Praxis II pedagogy tests, you will be expected to know theories, theorists, and operational terms that represent what is currently known about educational psychology. You will be expected to apply these theories to case histories and scenario readings.

Demonstrating Potential for Teaching Expertise and the Praxis II

According to Woolfolk (9/e, p.6), expert teachers possess certain attributes that support their classroom effectiveness. These attributes include knowledge of:
- subject matter.
- general teaching strategies that apply in all subjects.
- their students' backgrounds.
- the contexts in which students can learn.

The Praxis II tests your potential to become an expert teacher, by using case histories and short answer questions to assess working knowledge. According to the *Test at a Glance guide* for the *Principles of Learning and Teaching* assessments (0522, 0523, & 0524), short answer questions require the examinee to:

> "demonstrate understanding of the importance of an aspect of teaching, demonstrate understanding of principles of learning and teaching underlying an aspect of teaching, or recognize when and how to apply the principles of learning and teaching underlying an aspect of teaching."

An example of a case history found on the Praxis II Principles of Learning and Teaching, can be found on page 21 of the *Test at a Glance* document for test 0523, grades 5-9. (Go to the following website to download this Test at a Glance and others: http://www.ets.org/praxis/prxtest.html. If you do not already have Acrobat Reader, you can download it at the ETS site). In this example, the case of Mr. Jenner, a second-year teacher beginning his fourth week of instruction, is presented. Documentation includes Mr. Jenner's project plan, a supervisor's observation notes and transcripts, and transcripts of a conversation between Mr. Jenner and a colleague.

Sample questions follow the case history, along with a scoring guide. Scores range from 0 to 2:

- 0 indicates no appropriate responses to any part of the question
- 1 represents an answer with appropriate responses to part of the question
- 2 represents an answer with appropriate responses to all parts of the question, along with a demonstration of understanding of both the case history and the principles of learning and teaching outlined in the content categories covered in the test.

The *Test at a Glance* also presents two sample questions, along with responses to each representing scores of 0, 1, and 2. Below is the second sample question, along with a discussion of the sample responses receiving scores of 0, 1, and 2. The actual sample test questions can be found on page 25 of the *Test at a Glance* (0523).

Question 1. **Mr. Jenner's Project Plan (Document 1) demonstrates several aspects of effective planning. Explain TWO strengths in the Project Plan. Base your response on principles of planning instruction.**

Document 1: Mr. Jenner's Project Plan taken directly from page 21, *Test at a Glance* (0523).

World Cultures Panel Presentation

Objectives: Students will

1. Review and use concepts about world cultures
2. Demonstrate speaking and listening skills
3. Use creativity (art, literature, music, multimedia, objects)
4. Use higher-order thinking skills

Assignment:

1. You will work in assigned groups of five
2. Each group will select one culture from a list
3. The group will plan, gather information, and present a panel report to the class on the culture
4. Use the characteristics of a culture studied last week to organize your presentation
5. Include some use of art, literature, music, multimedia, or other cultural objects
6. All students must participate in group planning and presentation

Activities:

1. Presentation/discussion of assignment; video of effective panel from another class; assign groups
2. Group work: select culture; plan presentation, assign responsibilities

---

3. Group work: prepare presentations
4. Panel presentations
5. Writing assignment: comparison/contrast of cultures

Assessment:

1. Group work: individual and group grade
2. Panel presentation: individual and group grade
3. Writing assignment

Lets begin with a sample response receiving a score of 0. Although the *Test at a Glance* , presents the highest score first, we will to build up to the best; it gives us something to look forward to! The sample responses are taken directly from page 25 of the *Test at a Glance* (0523).

Sample response receiving a score 0: One aspect of effective planning that I have learned is always to make your unit plan or your lesson plan well organized and easy for you to follow and for others to understand. Many people may see your lesson plan - a mentor teacher, a supervisor, your principal - and the first impression they form of your teaching may come from the lesson plan. Mr. Jenner's Project Plan is very well organized, presented in clear outline form, and is easy to understand and follow.

Critique:
Woolfolk (p. 432) summarizes research on instructional planning:
- Planning influences what students will learn.
- Teachers engage in several layers of planning: year, term, week, day.
- Plans reduce, but do not eliminate, uncertainty in teaching.
- Teachers need wide ranging knowledge about students and their interests and abilities, subject-matter, instructional approaches, assessment, and how to adapt materials and resources for effective learning.
- There is no one model for effective planning

Looking back at the scoring criteria, a high score of 2 demands that the response answers the question asked. This response falls short in at least two ways. First, it addresses the organization of the plan, and certainly a well-organized plan is advantageous, but the respondent offers no evidence to support the claim of strong organization. No special insight about learning and teaching was provided in that aspect of the response. Second, a purpose of planning is to influence and advance student learning. This respondent fails to mention any effect that the plans will have on the learners. Instead, the response focuses on the anticipated effects of the plan on other educators. A good result requires that you demonstrate understanding of principles of learning and teaching. Let's look at the next sample response.

Sample response receiving a score 1: The Project Plan demonstrates aspects of effective planning. A very important feature of Mr. Jenner's planning is that he is building on prior knowledge. He tells the students that they are to use the characteristics of a culture studied the previous week to organize their presentations. When teachers link what has already been studied to a new task or a new concept, students have a much better opportunity for success. Building on prior knowledge is always to be desired in planning lessons, and Mr. Jenner does this well.

Critique:
This response is an improvement over the first one. The respondent accurately identifies Mr. Jenner's intention to build on the students' prior knowledge of culture to understand another culture. This response, however, has a few shortcomings that prevent it from receiving a score of 2. . First, the respondent suggests that Mr. Jenner builds on prior knowledge well, but there is no evidence of that in the case history. Second, the respondent offers no insight about the value of prior knowledge in learning. Third, the respondent identified only one strength of the plan, not two as requested. Although some may feel it is picky, it is best to follow verbatim questions asked, and answer all the question content as directly as possible.

Sample response receiving a score 2:
Mr. Jenner's Project Plan demonstrates several aspects of effective planning. His goals, assignment, activities, and assessment are closely related and support each other. For example, his objective of using creativity (art, literature, music, multi-media, objects) is directly supported by requirement #5 of his assignment. His objective of demonstrating speaking and listening skills, his requirement that all students must participate in group planning and presentation, and his assigning both an individual and group grade for the group work and the presentation support each other.

Critique: This response deserves a 2 because it answers the question in total. First, it identifies two strengths of the plan as called for in the question. First, the respondent asserts that there is an overall cohesiveness to the Project Plan, and offers evidence of that quality of effective planning. Second, the answer indicates that the respondent understands that planning should focus on student behavior instead of on teacher behavior.
Overall, this is a good response to the question because it addresses all parts of the questions, it offers evidence to support its assertions, and indicates an understanding of the role of plans in instruction. For additional guidance on the purposes and uses of planning, refer to Chapter 12 of your textbook.

Discrete multiple-choice questions

The remaining questions in the Praxis II Principles of Learning and Teaching series (0522-0524) are multiple-choice items assessing conceptual knowledge. They do not relate to the earlier case studies, but still test working knowledge. The first suggestion is for you study your textbook thoroughly, reviewing the key theories and concepts in preparation for the test. Go back to **Section 1: General Praxis Test Information**, and review the **test taking tips**. Also, be sure to familiarize yourself with the vocabulary and terms emphasized in the textbook. Play with the terms mentally, applying concepts learned in class and textbooks to real situations. For instance, many students have trouble understanding the concept of *negative reinforcement* . Essentially, they do not understand why negative reinforcement is just as likely as positive reinforcement to increase the likelihood of behavioral repetition. After all, how can something negative be positive? To appreciate the concept of negative reinforcement, you can evaluate daily activities for examples of positive and negative reinforcement. If, for example, you like calling home and speaking to your mother when you are feeling down, you have experienced a negatively reinforcing event. If calling Mom lifted your spirits, removing displeasure, the call was a negatively reinforcing event; it removed something that was not pleasant. Removing something unpleasant is just as reinforcing as adding something pleasant, isn't it? Life is filled with such simple examples of concepts learned in educational psychology; you just have to open your eyes to see them. Once you see them, your conceptual understanding will improve exponentially! Further, the better you can apply your knowledge to actual situations, the more likely will you be able to apply it to counterfactual situations encountered during a test like the Praxis. So **PRAX**TICE makes perfect!

PART THREE
PRACTICE TESTS

Case Histories

The following practice test and the corresponding answer key is intended to give you an idea of the types of questions the Praxis II pedagogy tests will present to you. A strong score on these tests requires conceptual knowledge of educational psychology. In this section, you will encounter several case histories with corresponding multiple-choice questions and constructed-response items. An active classroom is a complex environment, so the test items for each case history will cover a variety of the significant topics, concepts, and principles that Anita Woolfolk addresses in your textbook. The answer key for these questions is provided below. Although mastery of these items does not guarantee passing the Praxis II pedagogy tests, they will certainly enhance your preparation to tackle the challenge to come. It is suggested that you complete these items, and then compare your responses to the answers in the key. For those items you missed, review the appropriate sections in the text to find why you were not correct. Understand that errors are inevitable, and are a necessary part of learning.

Case History 1

Alana, a second grade teacher, expected an exciting, but exhausting school year. First, during the summer the school board "redistricted" the boundaries for each of the district's elementary schools. Over the past decade new apartment complexes and housing developments transformed the formerly rural school district into an upscale, suburban district. Alana's school, Mitchell Elementary School, always had a much higher percentage of students of lower socio-economic status (SES) students than the other schools in the district. With the redistricting, the school's new population would much more closely represent the district as a whole.

Second, the elementary schools were adopting a new language arts program. Reading and writing, speaking and listening would no longer be taught as isolated sets of skills. Instead, these skills would be learned through thematic, literature-based activities that required the use of multiple sets of skills (for example, writing a response to a speech). There was an orientation meeting at Mitchell for the new language arts program. The representative of the textbook publisher that produces the program proudly announced that a study revealed a statistically significant increase in standardized reading scores compared to all other competing programs.

In order to measure the effectiveness of the new program, the district would compare the results of this year's standardized tests with the results of the previous year's results. The comparison of scores would be published in the local newspaper.

1. The lower SES children that Alana taught over the years tended to score lower on the yearly achievement tests than higher SES children. Which of the following factors should this difference NOT be attributed to?
   a. learned helplessness
   b. cognitive deficits
   c. low teacher expectations
   d. low self-esteem

2. Based on research into the effects of SES on student achievement, which one of these effects could be safely predicted about the redistricting of the schools?
   a. A rise in standardized test scores for each of the district's schools
   b. A decrease in standardized scores for Mitchell Elementary School relative to the other district schools
   c. No significant change in standardized test scores in any of the schools
   d. A rise in the standardized scores of Mitchell Elementary School relative to the other schools

3. The statistically significant increase in scores that resulted from use of the new language arts program indicates that
   a. the results did not happen by chance.
   b. the new program is suitable for all students.
   c. the new program is the best available program.
   d. the results have been replicated in other testing situations.

4. The cause-and-effect nature of the study (i.e., use of the new program results in higher test scores) indicates that the study was which type in nature?
   a. correlational
   b. descriptive
   c. action research
   d. experimental

5. Some teachers argued that comparisons of school scores between last year's scores and this year's scores would be flawed. Which of these statements would BEST support their argument?
   a. Year-to-year achievement of students is impossible to measure with standardized tests.
   b. Much of the important learning that occurs in school is not measured by standardized tests.
   c. Standardized tests penalize minority students.
   d. The population in each school is dramatically different from a year ago.

Construct-a-Response: The administration of standardized tests and their uses often arouse much anxiety among parents. How would you explain the uses of standardized tests to a group of worried parents?

Case History 2

Katie is a fourth grade student in Josh Brown's class. Here is how her morning went one day.

8:45 - 9:00/ Upon entering the classroom, Katie and her classmates immediately put away their personal belongings, and put their homework in the homework box. Table by table, the children in the class hung their nametags on hooks by photos of various "free time" activities (e.g., board games, arts and crafts area, classroom library, computer center) Katie returned to her seat, reached into her desk, and took out her diary. Other classmates took out drawing pads or books of one type or another. The principal led the school in the Pledge of Allegiance, made the daily announcements for the students and teachers, and finally, he posed the daily brainteaser or riddle.

9:00 - 9:15/ While Katie was writing in her diary (and other students were drawing in pads or reading books), Mr. Brown took attendance and the lunch count. Next, he met with two students who had been having difficulties with each other. Katie couldn't tell exactly what occurred, but there seemed to be a lot of talking going on between Mr. Brown and the two students.

9:15 - 9:30/ "One of everybody's favorite times of the day," thought Katie. Mr. Brown read a chapter today from *Tim and Tess: Time Travelers* . (The Tim and Tess series was about two ten year-old detectives who traveled back in time to solve ancient mysteries, using the knowledge of the modern world.) Mr. Brown read aloud with lots of expression, accents, and dramatic flourishes. Katie and all her friends would read along silently (and sometimes chime in) from their own paperback copies of the book as Mr. Brown read aloud.

10:00 - 10:30 / Katie was beginning to see a pattern in the way Mr. Brown taught math. "Whenever we start a new topic, Mr. Brown teaches the whole class a new idea, and then he helps us do a lot of chalkboard problems. We do workbook assignments on our own, that he checks - sometimes he helps a couple of kids who are having trouble while we do the workbook pages, and he spends a lot of time reviewing stuff. Then the next day, he reviews it all, and he adds something a bit different. After a few days of that, he has us work on group projects. It starts to get a little boring, but then he usually does something neat. Like this Friday... each of the groups has to work on a real recipe that uses fractions, but no group will get the right measuring spoons. He said we'll have to use what we know about fractions to do the recipes the right way. And we have to explain how we did it. It's going to be fun. "

Katie got it right pretty much. A look at Mr. Brown's lesson plans for the next few days would reveal these objectives: a) Students will reduce 10 proper fractions to simplest terms in ten minutes with 90% accuracy; b) Students will match the following terms with their definitions with total accuracy: proper fraction, mixed fraction, improper fraction, numerator, denominator, common denominator; c) Students will use knowledge of fractions to complete a recipe when a complete set of measuring implements are unavailable (i.e., no group has a complete set of measuring implements and they must convert numerators and denominators to finish the recipe); d) Students will make a presentation that explains how they accomplished the task mentioned in (c) (e.g., mock interview, chart, story).

10:30 - 10:45/ Free time!! Katie went to the arts and crafts area and continued working on her weaving project. She hoped to have a potholder finished by the end of the week. Katie was getting wise to Mr. Brown (and so was everyone else). When there were no behavior problems during free time - and there almost never were - Mr. Brown would often extend it for five or ten minutes. And, she noticed, he did that a lot when the kids participated well during math.

10:45 - 11:45/ Mr. Brown was BIG into science. It was Katie's team's week to check the class weather station, log the data for the thermometer, barometer, wind speed and direction, check the clouds, and go on the Internet to report their data a some schools hundreds of miles away. (Katie was proud that she and the kids in the class made many of the weather instruments themselves.) And after all that, each team had to use the data to make a one-day and three-day weather report. When the weather activities were completed, Mr. Brown took the class outdoors because they were beginning a unit on the food web. The tasks for the next several days: catalogue and then identify the plants and animals on the school grounds.

11:45 - 12:00/ Get ready for lunch and RECESS!

6. Katie and her classmates know exactly what to do when they enter the classroom each morning. Mr. Brown clearly has devoted much attention to which aspect of classroom management?
   a. procedures
   b. rules
   c. activation
   d. time on task

7. Katie was quite interested in learning what was going on between the two students who were having problems with each other. As an effective classroom manager Mr. Brown would be most likely to
   a. publicly admonish the student more at fault for the problem in order to reinforce observational learning.
   b. privately impose a penalty on the offending student(s).
   c. impose a penalty before the charged emotions could dissipate.
   d. dismiss the problem and continue as usual.

8. Mr. Brown understands the impact that observational learning can have on student learning and behaviors, and he used observational learning effectively in his classroom. Observational learning is a major factor in which of these theoretical perspectives?
   a. constructivism
   b. social cognitive theory
   c. operant conditioning
   d. levels of processing theory

9. Katie's father, at conference time, mentioned that he and his wife delight in listening to Katie read each day's chapter. She incorporates accents and voicing

patterns that she hears from Mr. Brown. In this case Katie's parents are witnessing the influence of

    a. continuous reinforcement.
    b. vicarious incentives.
    c. observational learning.
    d. rule - e.g. method.

10. Re-examine the manner in which Mr. Brown introduces a new mathematics skill or concept to the class. Based on the instructional strategy that Katie described, when Mr. Brown introduced the unit on fractions, he worked from which perspective of instruction?

    a. student-centered
    b. teacher-centered
    c. guided discovery
    d. discovery

11. Mr. Brown endeavors to incorporate a variety of instructional taxonomies and levels into lessons and other activities. One of his objectives for the daily chapter reading is to help students "value" literature. This objective is associated with which taxonomy?

    a. cognitive
    b. psychosocial
    c. affective
    d. psychomotor

12. Re-examine the passage in the case history that discusses Mr. Brown's instructional objectives. Which of those objectives would be classified as behavioral objectives?

    a. b and d
    b. a and b
    c. b and c
    d. c and d

13. Which of those instructional objectives would be best described as cognitive objectives?

    a. b and d
    b. a and b
    c. b and c
    d. c and d

14. Prior to a reading of *Tim and Tess: Time Travelers*, Mr. Brown will often pose questions and comments to the students to help them break down the plot into pieces so they can understand the relationship between the characters, events, and setting. Which level of the cognitive taxonomy of objectives is Mr. Brown addressing with the questions and comments?

    a. analysis
    b. evaluation
    c. synthesis
    d. comprehension

15. Mr. Brown was adept at developing his students' motivation to learn. When he first incorporated "free time" into the daily schedule, he was confident that it would be well-received and trouble-free because he incorporated which one of these principles of intrinsic motivation into its design.

a. cognitive behavior management
b. incentives
c. self-determination
d. rewards

16. In planning the weather station and the learning tasks related to it, Mr. Brown emphasized real-life experiences, the integration of content areas (e.g., reading, mathematics, science), problem-solving activities, and group work. Such types of learning activities are associated with which major approach to instruction and learning?
    a. self-regulatory
    b. student-centered
    c. self-managed
    d. teacher-centered

17. As the principal walked through the school's hallways and cafeteria each day, he'd elicit answers from students about the daily brainteaser or riddle. The next morning a student who got it right would reveal the correct answer during the daily announcements. His goal was very simple. He wanted the students to pair pleasant events with attendance in school. This goal is associated with which of these theoretical perspectives?
    a. culturalism
    b. constructivism
    c. cognitivism
    d. classical conditioning

Construct-a-Response: Observational learning and modeling are important parts of Mr. Brown's instructional repertoire. What steps can a teacher take to optimize learning through observation and modeling?

Case History 3

After three sessions, 13-year old Nick was beginning to open up to Mrs. Snell, the school guidance counselor. Nick had only been in this school for a couple of weeks. He had attended *numerous* schools as a foster child. Finally, his aunt gained custody of him. Not all was well, however. Nick was having difficulties with his seventh-grade teachers, his classmates, and his schoolwork.

From Nick's point of view, the teachers were constantly criticizing him. "You're late again for homeroom...Please stop dreaming... Where's your homework... You didn't do this work properly..." and so on.

From Nick's point of view, the other kids were hostile. Sometimes they mocked the way he dressed. Kids would groan when he was assigned to one of their cooperative learning groups. (Other students had a difficult time reading his rushed, cramped handwriting and his poor spelling. And he was such a poor reader that he slowed the group's progress. And already Nick had one fight - with a boy who crossed his eyes to make fun of Nick's facial appearance.)

Mrs. Snell had a meeting with Nick's team of teachers. "Talk about someone who 'fell through the cracks'," remarked the lead teacher. "Take a good look at him. It looks like he has never seen a dentist. And I'd bet that he has never been to an eye doctor either." The teachers verified much of what Nick stated, albeit from a different perspective. "He's often lethargic or sleepy. Some kids were teasing him this morning. He was wearing a dirty, light cotton T-shirt - and here we are in a brutal cold snap."

The teachers also were quite concerned about Nick's poor academic performance. The lead teacher spoke, "We don't have much in the way of records for Nick. He's really bounced around a lot, and it looks like he never stayed at one school long enough for anybody to do any serious work with him. We're not sure whether his problems are due to the disruptions in his life, inferior instruction in inferior schools, or what other factors could be contributing to his problems. Each of us has begun keeping a folder of his work and a log of his behaviors. In about a week, when we feel we can better describe the patterns that we see, maybe we can meet again to discuss some strategies to implement to get this kid going in the right direction. In the mean time, let's have the school's learning specialist test Nick to determine what this kid knows and what his level of math and reading skills are."

"Sounds OK," responded Mrs. Snell. "And I'll also contact Nick's aunt and the state's child protection agency. It seems that she might need a hand, and perhaps the agency can get something going with regard to the health issues that you mentioned. All right... let's meet here a week from today."

18. Aggressive behavior has surrounded Nick (toward him and against him) during his first couple of weeks in the school. Which of these techniques would NOT be useful in dealing with aggressive classroom actions (e.g., name calling, bullying, punching)?
   a. Discuss the effects of antisocial actions.
   b. Teacher-modeling of non-aggressive conflict resolution
   c. Isolate victims and aggressors from the general class population
   d. Role play appropriate self-defense

19. Based on the signs observed by the educators who deal with Nick, which of these experiences likely has had the most profound effect on Nick's development?
   a. anorexia nervosa
   b. sexual abuse
   c. drug abuse
   d. physical neglect

20. The learning specialist will administer a set of tests to identify specific weaknesses in Nick's learning processes. These types of tests are known as _____ tests.
   a. formative
   b. aptitude
   c. diagnostic
   d. intelligence

21. When looking through Nick's thick confidential student folder, Mrs. Snell located an achievement test for Nick from second grade. The test indicated that Nick scored at the 87th percentile for reading comprehension. This scores indicates that Nick's
   a. correctly answered 87% of the test items.
   b. raw score was lower than 87% of the students in the norming sample.
   c. raw score was higher than 13% of the students in the norming sample.
   d. raw score was higher than 87% of the students in the norming sample.

22. The school psychologist tested Nick on an individual basis, and the test yielded an IQ score of 105. This IQ score is
   a. slightly below average.
   b. about average.
   c. not useful because IQ scores have no relationship with success in school.
   d. not useful because IQ scores typically swing dramatically during the middle school years.

23. From the perspective of Erikson's theory of psychosocial development, at his age Nick has probably entered the stage of Identity versus Role Confusion. The important events that help shape an individual's successful resolution of this stage are centered on
   a. acceptance of one's place in life.
   b. independence from others.
   c. love relationships.
   d. peer relationships.

24. There are times Nick's must impose penalties on him to maintain order in the classroom. When imposing penalties on students, good practice suggests that teachers
   a. remind the student in public that he has not kept his side of the bargain so that other students will pressure the offending student to conform.
   b. be certain that all students hear the verbal exchange between student and teacher so that all students benefit from the teacher's disciplinary message.
   c. avoid reestablishing a positive relationship with the students for a lengthy period in order to reinforce the teacher's distaste for the offensive behavior.
   d. delay discussions and interventions with the involved students until they are calmer and more objective.

Construct-a-Response: All the educators who deal with Nick agree that he suffers from a lack of self-esteem. What steps can the guidance counselor and Nick's team of teachers takes to enhance his self-esteem?

Case History 4

Ms. McHenry, principal, convened a meeting of the Student Assistance Committee (SAC). The SAC exists to help teachers solve problems with students that involve social, behavioral, academic, or emotional issues. This SAC consists of the principal, a guidance counselor, a learning disabilities specialist, a classroom teacher, and the teacher who makes a student referral to it.

The SAC members read the background information prepared by the teacher, Ms. Sterling. Prior to kindergarten, Alexander attended the school district's preschool program for children who display difficulties with cognitive, psychomotor, language/speech, social, or emotional development. A child study team (CST) evaluated Alexander, and on the basis of his speech, psychomotor, and emotional problems, it classified him as *Multiply Handicapped*, and an Individualized Education Plan was written for Alexander. At the end of the preschool year, the CST, the preschool teacher, and Alexander's parents had a conference to discuss his placement for kindergarten. They agreed that the least restrictive placement for Alexander would be a regular full-day kindergarten. The IEP stipulated that Alexander should receive services from a speech therapist, an occupational therapist (for his psychomotor problems), daily support in the Resource Room, and that he should have counseling sessions with a guidance counselor to address his anger problems and oppositional behavior. Most of the goals for Alexander were related to his behaviors. The IEP also stipulated that a classroom aide should assist Alexander's kindergarten teacher.

Ms. Sterling described the problems she was having with Andrew. For the first three or four weeks of school, Alexander was prone to severe temper outbursts. It did not take much to trigger one of these near tantrums - allowing another child to lead a line when Alexander expected to lead it could cause an incident. Not coincidentally, this behavior was occurring at a time when Alexander's pediatric psychiatrist was weaning him off a medication for hyperactivity for a switch to a medication to stabilize mood swings. These outbursts as well as Alexander's oppositional behavior made it quite difficult to establish routines and procedures with the class. but with the help of the aide, Ms. Sterling was able to accomplish that goal.

Eventually, the new medication, counseling sessions, consistent classroom discipline, and Ms. Sterling's keen gauging of Andrew's moods began to make a difference: fewer temper outbursts and less oppositional behavior. Other problems, however, began to emerge. Despite the assistance of an aide, the schedule of speech therapy, occupational therapy, resource room visits, and counseling sessions was having a negative effect on Alexander. He resented it when he had to leave the classroom (especially during an enjoyable activity) to go to one of these sessions. Ms. Sterling felt that these maneuvers were disrupting the good order of her classroom, and that the other students were suffering as a result.

"Are you having difficulties fulfilling any parts of the IEP?" "Yes," replied the teacher, "Well, for one, I simply don't have the time at the end of the day to send a daily report home to his parents. And that is causing a strain between Alexander's parents and me. The preschool class had seven children and two aides. I have twenty-four and one aide."

The members of the SAC began to brainstorm some ideas to assist Ms. Sterling.

25. The principle of *least restrictive placement* of students with special needs requires school districts to
    a. fully include students with special needs in regular classrooms.
    b. place special needs students in a limited number of regular classroom activities at first and regularly increase the time.
    c. place special needs students in as normal an educational setting as possible.
    d. provide a maximum level of support for a students with special needs.

26. Alexander's IEP must be
    a. accessible to the public upon request.
    b. updated on a yearly basis.
    c. validated in court with at least one parent/guardian present.
    d. revised when school personnel have difficulty fulfilling its provisions.

27. Alexander's behavior was a challenge to Ms. Sterling's classroom management skills. Which one of the following outcomes is NOT a goal of effective classroom management?
    a. the development of student self-control
    b. an increase in academic learning time
    c. a reduction of student-to-student verbalizations
    d. enhance student understanding of how to participate in classroom activities

28. The principal observed, "Based on the schedule I see here, it looks like Alexander is out of the kindergarten room more than he is in it. Would it be a good idea revise the IEP and reassign Alexander to a special education classroom, and have him go to the kindergarten just for specific learning activities - at least until his behavior improves dramatically?" The principal is pondering which type of special needs placement?
    a. mainstreaming
    b. cooperative teaching
    c. reciprocal teaching
    d. cognitive apprenticeship

29. Ms. Sterling realizes that it is not possible for Alexander to immediately reach the behavior goals specified in the IEP. Instead, she reinforced progress toward those goals. This technique is known as
    a. partial reinforcement
    b. extinction
    c. shaping
    d. Premack Principle

30. The guidance counselor realized that the assumption that the daily report needed to be *written* was irrelevant to the problem. He suggested that Ms. Sterling send home a daily chart, broken down into time segments that used icons (ex: happy faces, sad faces, angry faces, and so on) in place of a written report. The counselor's re-representation of this problem is an example of

a. means-ends analysis
b. translation
c. algorithmic analysis
d. schematized incubation

31. When first facing Alexander's refusal to leave the classroom for his other activities, Ms. Sterling employed strategies that had been effective in the past with other students. This type of problem solving approach is known as
    a. means-ends analysis
    b. functional fixedness
    c. reorganization
    d. schema driven problem solving

32. Ms. Sterling, after exhausting all other strategies that she could think of, decided to give Alexander a sticker each time he left the classroom peacefully. When Alexander collected five stickers, he could exchange them for a visit with the paraprofessional to the library for a book. Ms. Sterling is employing which type of reinforcement schedule?
    a. variable-ratio
    b. variable-ratio
    c. fixed-ratio
    d. fixed interval

33. Soon after Ms. Sterling began to present Alexander stickers for leaving the room peacefully, a couple of other children who also left the room for special purposes began to act out. Which of these major perspectives or theories would best offer an explanation for these behaviors?
    a. social cognitive theory
    b. attribution theory
    c. operant conditioning
    d. classical conditioning

Construct a Response: Emotional problems of the type that Nick displays can exhaust a teacher and undermine a pleasant classroom atmosphere. What disciplinary strategies might you implement to address inappropriate classroom behaviors?

Case History 5

The two U. S. history teachers could not have been more different in their instructional approaches. In Mr. Wolper's classroom the teacher was central. In most of his instructional activities he would explain the major trends, concepts, and events of U. S. history. He would usually prepare the students for a lesson by linking its theme to a familiar contemporary issue or controversy. The relationships among facts, events, and historical figures were explained in a well-organized, sequential fashion. A "Wolper" lesson, however, entailed far more than merely listening to a teacher. Students would use the principles and concepts that they encountered in lessons to analyze and understand present-day problems as well as those of a century ago. And, he often interspersed the lesson with questions to aid in understanding.

In Ms. McNally's classroom the students were central. She usually employed cooperative approaches to learning. She had a sophisticated knowledge of the uses of different cooperative techniques. For example, when introducing the students to a new chapter, she would often employ a strategy in which pairs of students took turns explaining, questioning, and elaborating information from the history textbook. One of the most popular strategies was the Webquest, a form of guided discovery learning in which teams of students use resources from the World Wide Web (and other non-Web resources) to develop unique solutions or interpretations to problems posed in a content area. The element of the Webquest that usually generated the most interest was the negotiations between Ms. McNally and the students over the design of the scoring rubric that would be used for grading the Webquest projects.

34. From time to time, Mr. Wolper would invite students to write anonymous comments about the quality of his instructional activities, including his lectures, questions, and explanations. He would analyze the comments, and use them to improve his performance. Mr. Wolper's effort at improvement is an example of
    a. integrative instruction
    b. selective review
    c. reflective practice
    d. bottom-up instruction

35. Mr. Wolper primarily saw himself as an "explainer," someone who helped students understand and apply the major principles and concepts that have shaped U. S. history. Mr. Wolper would generally use which type of thinking in his lessons?
    a. inductive reasoning
    b. concrete-operational reasoning
    c. deductive reasoning
    d. elective reasoning

36. Mr. Wolper usually began a lesson with an advance organizer. The primary purpose of this instructional device is to
    a. provide scaffolding and support for new information that will be encountered.
    b. stimulate cognitive conflict among the students
    c. remind students of the principles of effective learning.
    d. provide time for students to assemble into peer learning groups

37. Which one of these teacher behaviors is NOT a characteristic of student-centered instruction?
    a. Teachers allow wait time after posing questions.
    b. Teachers encourage student autonomy and initiative.
    c. Teachers provide time for students to discover relationships.
    d. Teachers emphasize extrinsic rewards for learning.

38. One disadvantage of cooperative learning is that
    a. students might reinforce each other's misconceptions.
    b. it is too difficult to implement in most classrooms.
    c. cooperative activities generally focus on lower-level cognitive objectives.
    d. cooperative learning is effective mainly for advanced students.

39. Critics of discovery learning suggest that it is often NOT an effective instructional strategy because
    a. students usually lack the motivation to discover relationships among concepts.
    b. students too frequently confuse deductive reasoning and inductive reasoning.
    c. discovery learning is suitable only for older students.
    d. students often lack necessary background knowledge and problem-solving skills.

40. A key element in the use of successful guided discovery learning is
    a. rewards that are offered at critical points in the discovery process.
    b. well-organized lectures that explain critical concepts.
    c. feedback that helps students make connections among pieces of information.
    d. scripted cooperation.

41. An advantage of elaboration in learning activities is that elaboration
    a. makes new knowledge more memorable by connecting it to existing knowledge.
    b. helps to strike a balance between creativity and rote learning.
    c. requires learners to compartmentalize skills and knowledge for efficient use.
    d. triggers activation of sensory buffers.

42. When using a scoring rubric, it is good practice to
    a. avoid showing students models of good work so that they are not likely to mimic that work.
    b. use the rubric to rank students so they can compare their work to others for feedback.
    c. include students in its design so that they understand the factors that determine quality work.
    d. prevent student peer-assessment because they tend to over rate each other's work.

Construct a Response: Other teachers were amazed at how well Mr. Wolper's students could remember and understand the complex events and concepts that they encountered in his course. Analyze Mr. Wolper's instructional techniques from the cognitive perspective. Explain why his approach to instruction is so effective.

Case History 6

Mr. Dressen retired at mid-year, and Mr. Zebrowski, the new principal at Wilson Elementary School, had an instant problem on his hands. He had just received notification from the state department of education that his school was on the verge of being classified as "needing improvement." The reading scores of the four third grade classes had been drifting lower for three years in comparison to state and national scores. An increasing number of students were qualifying for supplemental instruction. Not one student was classified as an advanced reader. This classification would result in a complete restaffing of the school, loss of community control of the school, and perhaps the loss of some school funding - not to mention the likely flight of higher performing students to other schools.

The tests were scheduled just a few weeks ahead, so there was little time for major adjustments. Mr. Zebrowski did employ a few tactics he hoped would give him the breathing room to make any major changes. First, he sent home a letter to parents in which he stressed that students should come to school well rested for the tests. Attached to the letter was a test schedule. If a parent certified with a signature that a child had 8 hours of sleep before each day of testing, the child would receive a free snack at the end of the week. Second, for each morning of the five-day test period, the school cafeteria had a special breakfast with nutritious, tasty meals for the students. Third, at the first day's breakfast Mr. Zebrowski announced a *Great Attitude* program. Each student who, according to the teacher, followed test directions carefully and worked without distracting others would be able to exchange a *Great Attitude* ticket for a small prize from the Treasure Chest in the principal's office. (Mr. Zebrowski was well aware that some people might criticize some of these steps, but he believed it was important to try to make an immediate impact.) Fortunately, there was a very modest uptick in the test scores. The drift toward lower scores had stopped - at least for one year, and the school had a temporary reprieve from sanctions.

Over the summer, Mr. Zebrowski took three steps that he believed would boost test scores over the long term. First, he assigned four teachers to the third grade who had strong credentials and reputations in the teaching of reading. Second, he scrapped the policy of heterogeneous (mixed) grouping of classes in that grade. The third grade classes now would be grouped homogeneously (i.e. similar ability) by reading scores from the state tests. (One class would contain the low-ability reading students, two classes would contain the middle-ability reading students, and one class would contain the high-ability reading students.) Third, he intended to implement a cognitive apprenticeship program in each class. The teacher would model a small number of strategies essential for successful reading comprehension. Gradually, and with the support of the teacher's tips, hints, cues, and encouragement, the students would assume the teacher's role, and apply these strategies independently in their own reading.

43. Mr. Zebrowski's use of incentives is a form of
    a. trait-induced motivation
    b. extrinsic motivation
    c. cognitively-grounded motivation
    d. intrinsic motivation

44. Which one of the following behaviors is NOT an element of cognitive apprenticeships?
    a. External support of student learning through coaching
    b. Rewarding students for successful learning with concrete rewards
    c. Student reflection on reasons for progress

d. Student exploration of new ways to apply newly acquired knowledge or skills

45. What would likely be a major problem with homogeneous grouping for the low ability students in Mr. Skowronski's plan for ability grouping?
   a. Less access to school resources than students in higher-ability groups
   b. Larger classes that will result in less individualized instruction
   c. Overstimulation of cognitive processes by teachers intent on higher test scores
   d. Tendency of teachers to emphasize lower-order cognitive skills at the expense of higher-order cognitive skills

46. In schools that employ within-class ability grouping, effective practice requires teachers to
   a. form groups on the basis of IQ test scores
   b. keep group memberships the same for the school year so that students can adjust to each other's cognitive preferences.
   c. assemble the groups so that members share similar learning styles.
   d. form and reform groups on the basis of current achievement.

47. Each of these descriptions is likely to be true of each of the expert teachers assigned to the third grade EXCEPT
   a. Accomplishes classroom routines automatically and with little conscious thought
   b. Looks for patterns when encountering instructional or behavioral problems
   c. Sticks firmly to plans no matter what event or diversion might occur
   d. Improvises explanations and generates new examples on the spot

Construct a Response: The use of various forms of ability-grouping has been criticized for many years, yet the use of ability-grouping persists. What are the various types of ability-grouping. What are their perceived benefits? What can teachers do to use ability-grouping most effectively? Why do many educational psychologists criticize the use of ability-grouping? What alternatives are there to ability-grouping?

Case History 7

After just three years of teaching Charlayne Hall had developed a strong reputation among the middle school's science teachers. Yes, she used the textbooks and supplemental materials that the publisher of the science program provided, but Charlayne preferred that her students engage in actual science investigations and discover science as much in the same way possible as scientists learn about science. This year she designed a project in which her classes examined the effects of weather and seasons on the plant and animal life in the pond in the public park adjacent to the school. She and the students, for instance, regularly visited the pond to sample the population of birds, bacterial activity in the water, and record the numbers and identities of specimens in the insect traps, and so on. Charlayne viewed her students as novice scientists, and one of her jobs was to immerse students in the practices, thinking, and language of science. For example, when a student team would be puzzled by unusual or unexpected data, she

---

would model the way scientists might think their way around and through the problem.

Alone among the science teachers Charlayne would, when feasible, bring poetry, visual arts, or music into science activities. She encouraged students to express their knowledge of science in novels ways. Most students stuck with the "tried and true" oral or written reports. But some students thought their knowledge could best be demonstrated through skits, drawings, or pantomime (and even once through a dance). The science department's chairperson believed Charlayne's approach to learning and instruction would be the most suitable science teacher for academically gifted students. The chairperson came to this conclusion because Charlayne encouraged such students to explore increasingly challenging and sophisticated biology topics while working in the same classes with their same-age peers.

Charlayne found that assessment and grading was more difficult for her than instruction. At first, she relied almost exclusively on the testing materials that accompanied the publisher's science program. As she matured and reflected on her approach to teaching, Charlayne, recognized that different approaches to assessment and grading had different advantages and disadvantages. Eventually she developed a sophisticated assessment and grading system that included traditional and authentic tests with contract grading and scoring rubrics.

48. Charlayne's approach to science instruction is MOST characteristic of which approach to learning?
     a. programmed learning
     b. vicarious learning
     c. cognitive apprenticeships
     d. peer tutoring

49. When Charlayne modeled the approaches scientists would take in attacking a problem, she demonstrated how to *predict, hypothesize, review, estimate* - thinking skills that the students had difficulty performing on their own. While Charlayne was available to provide tips, example, and cues the students were able to perform those tasks well enough to solve many of their problems. From Vygotsky's sociocultural perspective of learning, Charlayne was guiding the students in the
     a. site of situated learning
     b. zone of proximal development
     c. community of cognitive practice
     d. stage of formal operations

50. The incorporation of music, dance, poetry and other forms of expression into science activities suggests that Charlayne understands the implications of which view of intelligence?
     a. emotional intelligence
     b. genetically-determined
     c. constructive intelligence
     d. multiple intelligences

51. Which one of the following descriptions is TRUE of authentic tests?

    a. norm-referenced grading
    b. emphasizes breadth of knowledge more than depth
    c. maximizes comparisons among students
    d. entails self-assessment on the student's part

52. Which one of the following test formats is NOT considered a traditional form of testing?
    a. exhibitions
    b. fill-in items
    c. multiple-choice questions
    d. matching exercises

53. Take a second look at the approach that Charlayne's school takes to the teaching of academically gifted students. Educators refer to such a program as
    a. acceleration
    b. enhancement
    c. convergent instruction
    d. enrichment

54. Charlayne's contract system was designed to judge whether students' attained certain standards or benchmarks of knowledge and skills. This is a form of
_____ grading.
    a. percentage
    b. norm-referenced
    c. curved
    d. criterion-referenced

Construct-a-Response: The challenges that Charlayne faced in developing a useful grading system is one that teachers - novice and expert alike - continually address. What tips or guidelines would you give to teachers who face those challenges?

Case History 8

As a thirty-year veteran teacher, twenty years in kindergarten, Lisa Figueroa had a good reputation for identifying students who might have problems in school, and she was generally recognized as the teacher in the school with the most expertise in these areas. Two children in her class particularly attracted her attention, Sandra and Daniel. By mid-October, about six weeks into the school year, Lisa felt comfortable enough about her observations to contact the children's parents for conferences. Each student was having difficulties with similar areas of school, but for different reasons.

Sandra
Sandra, Lisa explained to her mother, had a difficult time with handwriting, language activities, and arts and crafts activities. Sandra tended to rush through these activities - jumping ahead before the next set of directions were given. Activities that required practice tended to frustrate her. Sandra frequently interrupted other people while they were talking, had a difficult time taking turns, got into many quarrels with classmates, rocked in her seat quite a bit, and was easily distracted from learning activities. Lisa had to redirect Sandra to the task at hand frequently

---

Sandra's mother said that Sandra was like that in preschool. Often when she picked up Sandra after work, she would be sitting in the "time out" chair for one infraction or another of the rules. At home, she tended to flit from one plaything to the next and the living room was always a mess. Sandra was always outgoing and eager to make new friends, but she seemed to wear out her friends before too long

Daniel
Daniel, Lisa explained to his parents, had difficulty with handwriting, language activities, and arts and crafts activities. He tended to do these tasks very slowly, and he needed frequent reminders about what to do. Often he would sit in his chair seemingly as if he had never heard any directions to a task. His grasp of a pencil or crayon was awkward, and his hand was unsteady - even for a five-year old - as he used those writing tools. His figures were undeveloped compared to classmates. Daniel had a hard time recalling information from the stories that Lisa read to the children. Daniel did not have many friends in the class, but he did not have any enemies either

Daniel's parents were disappointed by Lisa's report. They mentioned that he seemed to attain several of the major developmental milestones (e.g., beginning to talk and walk). In fact, they enrolled him at the nearby preschool program a year later than his neighborhood peers because he was not yet toilet-trained. They mentioned that he was probably a "late bloomer," and as evidence they pointed to his vast knowledge of dinosaurs.

Lisa had a couple of strategies that she planned to use with Daniel and Sandra. First, she planned to seat him at a table with a couple of the more mature students - ones who had superior social and learning skills. Second, she also planned to use a signal for each of the students to prompt them when it was important to pay careful attention to directions. Third, when she gave directions to the students, she would ask each of them to repeat or paraphrase those directions. Lisa indicated to the parents that she would discuss each situation with the school's students assistance committee to design more interventions for each child.

55. Sandra is sensing that she is not as successful in many of classroom activities as her classmates. If she does not experience a sense of accomplishment during these early years of school, she may not successfully resolve which of Erikson's stages of psychosocial development?
    a. Industry versus inferiority
    b. Initiative versus guilt
    c. Identity versus role confusion
    d. Ego integrity versus despair

56. During literature activities, Lisa often poses questions that require the students to take the perspective of a storybook character. Students who can perform this task are employing which type of thinking?
    a. sensorimotor

b. preoperational
c. concrete operational
d. formal

57. The inability of a young child to understand experiences from the points of view of other people is known as _____.
   a. semiotic thought
   b. goal-directed thought
   c. egocentric thought
   d. affective thought

58. When teaching students who employ preoperational thought, it is advisable to
   a. present problems that require logical thinking.
   b. pose many hypothetical questions.
   c. provide opportunities to employ abstract reasoning.
   d. use concrete props as often as possible.

59. When Daniel realizes that he is not performing as well as his classmates, he folds his arms on the table, cradles his head in them, and sobs in embarrassment. Which stage in Erikson's theory of psychosocial development might Daniel not have resolved satisfactorily before he attended kindergarten?
   a. Basic trust versus mistrust
   b. Autonomy versus shame/doubt
   c. Identity versus role confusion
   d. Industry versus inferiority

60. Sandra's classroom and home behaviors are indicative of which condition?
   a. Attention Deficit/Hyperactivity Disorder
   b. a learning disability
   c. oppositional behavior
   d. cooperative dysfunctional disorder

61. Daniel's classroom behaviors and his history are indicative of which condition?
   a. Attention Deficit/Hyperactivity Disorder
   b. a learning disability
   c. oppositional behavior
   d. cooperative dysfunctional disorder

62. Lisa hoped that the more-capable students who sat the same tables as Sandra and Daniel would be able to provide valuable assistance with certain tasks. This type of assistance is known as _____.
   a. accommodation
   b. equilibration
   c. scaffolding
   d. assimilation

63. When Lisa was working with Daniel in his *zone of proximal development* for a learning task, she would be likely to
   a. offer tips, clues, or hints to assist his learning.
   b. pose questions that caused cognitive conflict.
   c. rehearse previously learned tasks.
   d. rely on vicarious experiences.

64. One morning Sandra caused two injuries to classmates. Sandra accidentally scratched Jared's eye when she flapped her hands when imitating a bird while playing a classroom game. Later, she elbowed Tim while in line when he said that he was "not Sarah's friend" because she cut in front of him while lining up. Sarah was visibly upset for hurting Jared, but she only produced a perfunctory apology to Tim. From Kohlberg's perspective, Sarah would be at which level of moral reasoning?
    a. conventional
    b. preconventional
    c. postconventional
    d. sensorimotor

Construct a Response: What are the major signs of learning disabilities during the school years (i.e., primary, elementary, middle school, and secondary grade levels), and what kinds of interventions does research support?

Case History 9

Heather was thrilled to be hired as a language arts teacher in the middle school that she attended a dozen years before. The building looked much the same, but the school population was much more economically, racially, ethnically, and linguistically diverse than it had been little more than a decade ago. From Heather's point of view, she faced three major challenges. First, she wanted to make sure that her instruction was culturally inclusive. Second, Heather wanted to make sure that students for whom English was not the first language would receive the most effective instruction and support that she - who was monolingual - could provide. Third, she wanted to make sure that each student no matter what his or her background should feel respected and accepted by every member of the class.

65. Research into the relationship between socioeconomic status (SES) and school achievement suggests that poverty
    a. plays little role in school achievement.
    b. has its greatest influence during the preschool years.
    c. has little effect on English-speaking students.
    d. has its greatest influence during high school.

66. Which of these explanations is NOT considered a legitimate reason for the poor achievement of many lower-SES students?
    a. poor health care
    b. cultural deficits
    c. academic tracking
    d. learned helplessness

67. When researchers compare differences in tests of cognitive ability among ethnic groups who are at the same SES level, they find that
    a. differences in cognitive abilities diminish.
    b. there are no differences statistically.
    c. gaps in cognitive abilities increase.
    d. all differences can be attributed to

68. Heather was diligent in selecting instructional and supplementary materials that exposed the students to a wide variety of cultural and ethnic experiences. This element of multicultural education is known as
   a. withitness.
   b. overlapping landscapes.
   c. cultural climatization.
   d. content integration.

69. Heather often incorporated cooperative learning into the set of instructional activities because many students came from backgrounds in which cooperative behaviors were emphasized over competitive behaviors. This element of multicultural education is known as
   a. face-to-face interaction.
   b. individual accountability.
   c. equity pedagogy.
   d. associative learning.

70. Research indicates that higher degrees of bilingualism are correlated with increased
   a. functional fixedness.
   b. poverty.
   c. creativity.
   d. cognitive deficits.

71. Experts in multicultural educators caution teachers
   a. that learned helplessness is NOT possible to overcome.
   b. to employ tracking for lower-SES students during middle school years.
   c. That students with limited proficiency in English suffer from a cultural deficit that must be addressed to boost achievement.
   d. To consider that students are members of multiple groups that each influence behavior in a variety of ways.

72. Heather is developing a culturally relevant approach to teaching. Which of these items is NOT a component of such an approach?
   a. present accomplishments of members of various ethnic groups.
   b. encourage students to ignore racist or bigoted messages.
   c. communicate regularly with parents/family members of students.
   d. Get to know the customs and traditions of students.

73. Heather saw that many of her students did not understand the informal or tacit rules for participation in her classroom. Of these techniques, which would be the LEAST effective in promoting appropriate classroom participation?
   a. Use cues to signal when rules for participation will change.
   b. Demonstrate the appropriate participatory behaviors for various situations.
   c. Make participation rules clear and unambiguous.
   d. Employ a "praise and ignore" approach to inappropriate classroom participation.

74. A few of Heather's students speak a dialect of English. To promote her students' academic achievement, Heather would be advised to
   a. employ a "drill and practice" to help students learn standard pronunciation.

b. encourage the parents of the students to use standard English exclusively in their   homes.

c. provide students with practice with feedback in using standard English.

d. respond to students only when they use standard English.

75. Many educational psychologists caution teachers about the instructional implications of learning styles research in diverse classrooms because

a. there is no evidence of differences in learning styles among ethnic groups.

b. the validity of some learning styles research is in question.

c. teachers cannot accommodate their teaching to a variety of learning styles in the classroom.

d. students naturally adjust their learning styles to the teacher's expectations.

Construct a Response: Given that the school population of this country is likely to continue to diversify ethnically and racially over the next several decades, what strategies can a teacher employ to establish a culturally relevant environment in his or her classroom?

Answer Key

Case History 1
1. b (Chapter 5)
2. d (Chapter 5)
3. a (Chapter 5)
4. d (Chapter 1)
5. d (Chapter 14)
Construct a Response:
(Chapters 14 & 15)

Case History 2
6. a (Chapter 11)
7. b (Chapter 11)
8. b (Chapter 9)
9. c (Chapter 9)
10. b (Chapter 12)
11. c (Chapter 12)
12. b (Chapter 12)
13. d (Chapter 12)
14. a (Chapter 10)
15. c (Chapter 10)
16. b (Chapter 12)
17. d (Chapter 6)
Construct a Response:
(Chapter 9)

Case History 3
18. c (Chapter 11)
19. d (Chapter 3)
20. c (Chapter 15)
21. d (Chapter 14)
22. b (Chapters 4 & 14)
23. d (Chapter 3)
24. d (Chapter 11)
Construct a Response:
(Chapter 3)

Case History 4
25. c (Chapter 4)
26. b (Chapter 4)
27. c (Chapter 11)
28. a (Chapter 4)
29. c (Chapters 4 & 6)
30. b (Chapter 8)
31. d (Chapter 8)
32. d (Chapter 6)
33. a (Chapter 9)
Construct a Response:
(Chapter 11)

Case History 5
34. c (Chapter 1
35. c (Chapters 8 & 12)
36. a (Chapter 8
37. d (Chapter 12)
38. a (Chapter 13)
39. d (Chapter 12)
40. c (Chapter 8)
41. a (Chapter 7)
42. c (Chapter 5)
Construct a Response:
(Chapter 7)

Case History 6
43. b (Chapters 6 & 10)
44. b (Chapter 9)
45. d (Chapter 4)
46. d (Chapter 4)
47. c (Chapters 1 & 8)
Construct a Response:
(Chapter 4)

Case History 7
48. c (Chapter 12)

49. b (Chapter 2)
50. d (Chapter 4)
51. d (Chapter 15)
52. a (Chapter 15)
53. c (Chapter 4)
54. d (Chapter 15)
Construct a Response:
(Chapter 15)

Case History 8
55. a (Chapter 3)
56. c (Chapter 2)
57. c (Chapter 2)
58. d (Chapter 2)
59. b (Chapter 3)
60. a (Chapter 4)
61. a (Chapter 4)
62. c (Chapter 2)
63. a (Chapter 2)
64. a (Chapter 3)
Construct a Response:
(Chapter 4)

Case History 9
65. b (Chapter 5)
66. b (Chapter 5)
67. a (Chapter 5)
68. d (Chapter 5)
69. c (Chapter 13)
70. c (Chapter 5)
71. d (Chapter 5)
72. b (Chapter 5)
73. d (Chapter 11)
74. c (Chapter 5)
75. b (Chapters 4 & 5)
Construct a Response:
(Chapter 5)

eferences

Educational Testing Service (2001). The Praxis Series Tests at a Glance: Education. Princeton, New Jersey: Educational Testing Service.

Educational Testing Service (2001). Your Guide to Registering for the Praxis Series. Princeton, New Jersey: Educational Testing Service.

Woolfolk, A. (2003). Educational Psychology, 9th Edition. Boston: Allyn & Bacon.